MW00614878

BIG AL MINDSET SERIES

HOW TO GET
MOTIVATED
IN
60 SECONDS

The Secrets to Instant Action

KEITH & TOM "BIG AL" SCHREITER

How to Get Motivated in 60 Seconds

© 2021 by Keith & Tom "Big Al" Schreiter

Published by Fortune Network Publishing

PO Box 890084

Houston, TX 77289 USA

Telephone: +1 (281) 280-9800

BigAlBooks.com

ISBN-13: 978-1-956171-01-3

CONTENTS

PREFACE

This seems a bit cruel but …

The universe does not care about our goals, wishes, needs, wants, and desires.

It doesn't care if we think something should be fair.

It only cares if we do what is required. It is pretty heartless.

Reality can be harsh. We wish we could sit in a chair, be positive, chant affirmations, and benefit from the vibrational riches of the universe. Imaginary worlds are fun to daydream about.

But we are adults now. It's time to move on to a more realistic awareness of our world.

There are three things we need to succeed in our adult world:

1. Clear focus on what we want. That "focus" thing sounds hard. No one taught a brain focus class in school. We don't even have a user manual for this. But this is something we feel we can do.

2. Skills to get what we want. Yes, we might have to learn a completely different set of skills than we learned in school. We've learned skills before. This is doable.

3. Motivation to get started. Oh. Ouch. This step is always the hardest.

How do we activate this all-important motivation step?

Do we need to tap into that mythical willpower other people talk about?

If we had willpower, we wouldn't be reading this book. We would be levitating on a stage while the audience stares in awe and worships the ground beneath us.

For us mere mortals, we will need much more than willpower to kickstart our motivation. So let's get started on our journey to motivation.

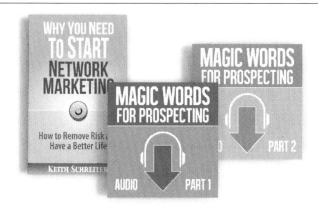

GETTING STARTED IS THE HARDEST PART.

We know what to do.

We know how to do it.

… and we still don't do it.

We don't need more instructions; we need the motivation to get started.

We say: "Look at our bank balance! I didn't know negative numbers got that big."

Our brain says: "Not our fault. Nothing to see here. Keep moving."

We say: "But won't the bank want payment on at least one of these loans?"

Our brain says: "We have other priorities. Our Netflix subscription fee won't pay itself! Starbucks isn't free, you know."

We say: "Time to get motivated. I am getting out of bed. I will call my prospects. This is the Monday that will change my life!"

Our brain says: "Whoa! Aren't you the rebel this morning? Nice try, loser. Behave or I will deploy the procrastination laser on your remaining brain cell."

We say: "I proclaim to the Universe, this time I will get into action!"

Our brain says: "You expect me to talk to the Universe? You are delusional."

The morning sun dims. Ominous clouds fill the sky. The Universe prepares to strike us dead for trying. And then a booming voice from above announces, "Here is your sign!"

A flash of lightning. Thunder. Snapping trees. Smoke. Sparks. The power goes off. The smell of burnt electrical wiring fills our bedroom.

Our brain says: "Who nuked the power? Are you trying to kill us? We are going to end up in the emergency room. Summoning the angry dark forces of the universe by attempting motivation is crazy. Hide under the covers! Avoid thinking! Try losing a few thousand brain cells!"

We say: "Whoa! Thinking is overrated. No more motivation. Re-engage autopilot."

And that is why we don't get motivated or take action.

"AN OBJECT IN MOTION TENDS TO STAY IN MOTION."

We may remember this from our grade school science class.

"An object in motion tends to stay in motion."

-- Sir Isaac Newton, 1687.

Our three-year-old escapes our grip ... and runs. And runs and runs. Fast. How do kids run so fast? We feel as if we are chasing them in slow motion.

Objects in motion tend to stay in motion. Our three-year-old won't stop running despite our begging.

In science class, we learn if we roll a ball along the ground, surface friction eventually slows our ball. But it takes a long time.

We don't expect our ball to suddenly stop. An object in motion tends to stay in motion. We want to be that object in motion.

It is the same with our personal motivation. Once we get started, it's easy to continue.

But getting started? That is the challenge!

Moving from zero to action takes effort.

If we get out of our chair and put on one running shoe ... we are in motion. It will be easier to stay in motion and continue.

Don't worry about the goal of getting out the door and on to the running track. It will be easier once we are in motion. The first step is the most important.

And what stops us from taking that first step?

- Uncertainty.
- Lack of belief.
- Addiction to our current dopamine.
- No energy.
- Mind games.

And ... the big reason. Here it comes.

"AN OBJECT AT REST TENDS TO STAY AT REST."

-- Sir Isaac Newton, 1687.

Yes, Sir Isaac knew his physics.

It takes a lot of effort to start.

That is why we feel glued to the sofa while mindlessly watching television. Objects at rest tend to stay at rest. We know how much effort it will take to move, and we decide to stay at rest.

Unfortunately, this applies to all areas of our lives.

This is why we delay our homework. Why we put off difficult decisions. Why we wait until the last minute to do unpleasant tasks. Our mind decides it is easier to stay where we are, and not to take on that humongous task of getting into action.

Can't relate? Well, let's look at a few examples.

- Staying in bed after our alarm goes off.
- Deciding to exercise tomorrow instead of today.
- Playing a few more computer games before starting our homework.
- Accepting that ironing clothes is overrated.
- Convincing ourselves we are too tired to exercise.
- Putting off washing the car until the weekend.
- Refusing to start a task until we feel better.
- Deciding our income tax preparation can be done later.

Our list can go on and on. Getting started, that first step, is the hardest thing for us to do.

Motivation is easier once we are in motion. But it is the first 60 seconds that makes the difference. We have to get in motion first.

This book is our guide to mastering those first 60 seconds.

DOES OUR BRAIN'S MOTIVATION GO ON HOLIDAY?

On the sofa, surrounded by snacks, remote control ready, smart-phone loaded with social media … we enter full "couch potato" mode.

Our entrepreneur mind reminds us that we should:

- Make phone calls.

- Follow-up with our prospects.

- Set more appointments.

- Work on our skills.

- Reach out for more referrals.

But what happens?

We feel the weight of 1,000 donuts holding us down. We can't move. We barely have the energy to press the buttons on our remote control.

Do we have goals? A vision board? A "why until we cry" reason to work this business?

Yes!

But we are still on the sofa.

Now, what are we going to do about it?

Will we decide to continue being victims of our minds?

Of course not. We want to fix this problem.

Every human faces this challenge of motivation. Motivation is easy once we are in "flow" and things are going well.

But ...

Those first few seconds make all the difference in the world. If we can manage those first few seconds and create instant momentum, motivation will work like they say it will in the textbooks.

If we don't skillfully manage those first few seconds, motivation will elude us. Our motivation suffers a head-on collision with procrastination. The laws of nature will control our brains and we talk ourselves out of taking action.

Remember Sir Isaac Newton's laws of motion?

- "An object in motion tends to stay in motion."
- "An object at rest tends to stay at rest."

So instead of putting up more vision boards or chanting affirmations, let's learn some hardcore skills and shortcuts to get motivated fast.

THE MOTIVATION HORMONE.

Feeling lazy? Unmotivated? Uninspired?

Consider drugs.

Dopamine is a man-made drug that we create inside our bodies. Think of dopamine as our motivation hormone.

More dopamine means more energy, a better attitude, a positive viewpoint, sharper focus and concentration.

Oh, and we have other hormones we can add to our motivation stockpile. Consider adding endorphins, oxytocin, and even serotonin. Our bodies are a pharmaceutical factory.

How do we activate these motivation hormones?

Let's think about this. Can we remember when these hormones made us feel better? Can we remember when missing these hormones made us feel worse? Let's look at some examples.

7:45, Saturday morning. Our ten-year-old selves jump out of bed thinking, "Saturday! No school. Morning cartoons. Playing with my friends. Weekend happiness!"

Our ten-year-old hormone-drugged brain commands energy and action. Motivation on steroids! Plus, ten-year-olds don't worry about the future. Monday seems years away.

And the flip side?

6:15, Monday morning. Our 40-year-old selves turn off the alarm and think, "Ugh." Not enough energy for more thoughts.

Our brain knows that Monday kicks off five days of job-induced depression. Well, not for everyone. Some people love their jobs. But for the majority of people? The Monday morning alarm feels as pleasant as dental surgery and tax audits.

Where are those helpful hormones? They are hiding. Monday mornings depress them, too.

Hormone Strategy #1: Mindset.

We want to reframe our Monday mornings. What can we do to make Monday mornings feel better in our minds?

How about food? Can we arrange to have our favorite breakfast of all time every Monday morning? Something so good we look forward to it? Maybe it is French toast and a special gourmet sausage, or whatever strikes your fancy.

Anything we can do to make our minds produce more happy hormones will help.

Hormone Strategy #2: Go to sleep earlier.

Sleep helps restore our hormone reserves. Lack of sleep makes us cranky and irritable. It also means we won't have enough happy hormones to deal with our attitude.

If Monday mornings become our biggest motivation challenge, going to sleep early on Sunday evening will help.

Hormone Strategy #3: Sunlight.

Think of the difference between waking up in total darkness, and waking up in sunlight. Sunlight lifts our moods.

To keep higher levels of motivation throughout our day, we want to get outside when we can. We want the sunlight to trigger more of these happy hormones in our systems.

What if we live in a place with depressing weather? Get a sun lamp. Sad weather doesn't have to control our moods.

Hormone Strategy #4: Meditation.

We don't have to go abroad and sit in a lotus position while humming.

A few minutes of peace in our minds make the difference. Here is how we can start.

Take three minutes. Relax. Let our minds wander. Don't concentrate or think. Just wander. Now is the time to be mentally lazy. Yes, lazy. This is easy. The happy hormone laboratories in our brains love this. When we finish, we have more motivation for taking action in our lives.

Want to make this more effective? Background music and free meditation apps are everywhere. Why not find one we like?

Hormone Strategy #5: Read something uplifting.

When we read, we identify with the characters we're reading about. If our favorite character overcomes adversity, we feel as if we overcame the same adversity. This results in a happy hormone release.

Books can motivate us to want more and do more. And as an extra benefit, we can learn new skills from books that make us even better at getting what we want. Success breeds success.

Hormone Strategy #6: Music.

Humans love music. Why? Because music helps us release happy hormones.

Some music will work better than other music. The music from our teenage years can leave a big impression.

We can do a two-stage method with music.

First, find fun, upbeat music that makes us smile. Got a particular song in mind? Great.

Second, play this song before we start working on the task we need to accomplish.

Over time, our minds will pick up a pattern. Our minds love routine. Routine means no thinking or judging, just doing what comes next. We play the song, our brains create some hormones, and now we are ready for action.

Remember Pavlov's dogs? He trained their brains by ringing a bell before he fed them. Then, Pavlov could cause the dogs to drool any time he wanted by ringing that bell. We can train our brains to react the same way.

Hormone Strategy #7: Food.

Yeah! Food! Who doesn't like food?

Can our food choices affect our hormones and motivation? Yes.

Let's talk about donuts. Imagine we have a donut addiction. The combination of extreme sugar and fat brings pleasant thoughts to our brains. How is our motivation now? We can walk uphill, in the rain, for an hour to get to our donut fix.

But there is a dark downside. After consuming a dozen donuts, how do we feel? Sluggish, tired, and unmotivated. This is truly a "Dr. Jekyll & Mr. Hyde" type of food. The ultimate hormone manipulator.

Here are some foods others find to help with their happy hormones for motivation. Which of the following could we add to our day for motivation?

- Chili peppers. For some, instant energy. For others, scorched mouths and heartburn.
- Coffee. Obvious. Try iced, donut-flavored coffee for an extra treat.
- Green tea.
- Any health food that uses "power" as part of its name.
- Almost anything with caffeine.
- Our favorite food.
- Dark chocolate. A serving of dark chocolate gives me superpowers. And some days I need extra superpowers. I eat a lot of dark chocolate.
- Supplements. Energy drinks. Herbs. Vitamins. All have energy claims.
- Nuts and seeds.

Overeating? Avoid! Avoid! A recipe for disaster.

Remember our visits to Grandma's house? To show her love, she fed us three times our daily limit. Grandma does this to keep us around longer, because one hour later, we can't even move.

Can we combine food with other strategies? Of course!

Imagine we have difficulty making sales phone calls. Before our calling sessions, why not turn on our favorite uplifting music, set out a bowl of dark chocolate near the phone, open the curtains to let the sunlight in, and allow our happy hormones to take over?

Does exercise induce procrastination? My exercise consists of walking. Not thrilling. Not exciting. But popcorn is my favorite food. Now, I only eat popcorn while on my daily walks. More on that later.

A bit of high-caffeine dark chocolate, an upbeat song, fresh popcorn in the machine, and I am ready for my walk. I then listen to science lectures while walking to make the exercise extra-special for me. It takes a lot to get me to exercise.

Hormone Strategy #8: Humor.

When we laugh, our happy hormone production goes into overdrive. This is the time to feed our sense of humor.

Can we find videos of people doing stupid things? How about some funny cat videos? Standup comedy clips of our favorite comedian? Do we have a favorite cartoon series we love?

When we laugh, our brain releases our happy hormones. We feel better. Our motivation goes up. This isn't rocket science.

Laugh. Laugh a lot. It works.

Hormone Strategy #9: Exercise.

First, a disclaimer. Exercise does create happy hormones. But getting the motivation to actually get off the sofa and start the exercise is the hard part. Let's focus on getting started.

Step #1. Pick an exercise we love to do. If playing basketball with our friends is fun, we won't need extra motivation to start. If walking to the donut shop feels great, starting won't be a problem. For me, jogging in circles and ending up where I started doesn't qualify as something I love to do. Pick an exercise that is fun.

Step #2. Enjoy the exercise. Be in the moment. Some runners report a "runner's high" within minutes of starting their runs. Keith, a lover of running, experiences this often. Me? I've never experienced this "runner's high" because I don't run. For me, it is only a rumor.

Step #3. Don't overdo the exercise. Keep some energy reserved for the task we need to do next.

Here is an example.

Step #1: Go shopping. We love to shop. It won't be hard to motivate us to get to the shops. We love this exercise.

Step #2: Find a bargain. Instant dopamine.

Step #3: Stop shopping before we get exhausted. We want to preserve some of that energy for our next task.

Okay, now that we have our hormones working for us, what's next?

A BRIEF HISTORY OF OUR NEAR-IMPOSSIBLE TASK.

Our minds run our lives. And they mess with us daily.

Let's look at how our minds operate. It seems that each of us got a mind at birth, but no operator's manual. Do we see the problem? This is going to be ugly.

Here is a simplification of what goes on.

We have a conscious mind. We think with our conscious mind. It can have one thought at a time. It's easily distracted. It goes to sleep at night. It gets tired.

We also have a subconscious mind. It does everything except handle our current conscious thoughts. It runs on automatic programs that we have from birth or learn along the way. We don't have to think to make our heart beat again. We don't walk by saying, "Left foot, then right foot."

Everything we do is on autopilot except our current conscious thought.

So which part of our brain runs our lives? The subconscious mind, of course. We are a collection of automatic programs going through life with brief moments of consciousness.

Here is the deal:

1. Our conscious mind thinks it is in control, but it isn't.

2. Our subconscious mind is in control, but it doesn't think. It only executes its automatic programs.

Our automatic programs can work against us and keep us from motivation. And that explains our challenge. Here is an example.

The conscious mind says: "I need to get in shape. I will go jogging."

The subconscious mind says: "No. I don't think so."

The conscious mind says: "I will look better if I get in shape."

The subconscious mind says: "My #1 program is survival. This program keeps us alive. It has worked so far by keeping us on the sofa. Don't mess with what works."

The conscious mind says: "I have willpower. I can do this. I can go jogging."

The subconscious mind says: "Seems too dangerous to me. We might get attacked by a lawnmower or random garbage can if we go outside. Let's stay safe right here and watch television."

The conscious mind says: "I give up. I used up all my energy talking to you."

The subconscious mind says: "Here is a cat video you can watch."

Think of our **conscious** mind as the dreamer, someone with the best intentions, but no power. Think of our **subconscious** mind as the doer, who ignores the weak little voice of the conscious mind.

This is why we have to use hacks, shortcuts, and strategies to deal with our all-controlling subconscious minds. We may not be able to control our subconscious minds, but we can intelligently influence them.

Let's see what we can do.

CONCLUSIVE PROOF.

People who take action do better than people who merely take notes. Who would have guessed?

Further research exposes another truth.

People taking action do better than people who only think about it.

Shocking!

Clearly the point of motivation is to get us into action.

So how can we put these breakthrough findings to work?

Suppose we relax on our easy chair. Bottles of beer and giant bags of chips surround us. The 10-hour streaming of our favorite television series is about to begin. Nice.

A vague, nagging memory of our morning goal comes to mind. We told ourselves, "Tonight, when I return from work, I will go jogging. And later, I will start to work on my taxes."

What will we choose?

To rationalize, of course. And then the conversation begins.

We say: "I am in the top 97% of all income earners. That is pretty good. I am doing better than the bottom 3%. Taxes? Not a priority until next week. And I need at least 15 uninterrupted hours to concentrate on that task. Not enough time this evening. My jogging shoes? Yeah, I see them all the way across the room. That is far. And I haven't planned a running route yet. That takes time. Work was exhausting. Certainly my health would improve if I had more recovery time."

Done. Our procrastinating brain throws a party and cheers, "We won again! Seven days in a row! Couch time forever!"

This feels familiar because we do it so often. Rationalizing becomes a habit. The longer we "think about" something, the longer we stay where we are. Thinking is procrastination. Rationalizing is nothing more than prolonged procrastination.

The #1 reason for personal and business failure?

Failure to start.

We can defeat the #1 reason for failure by taking our first step forward. One step.

The good news is that we only need enough willpower for the first step. After the first step, we have momentum. It is easier to continue.

Want to go for a walk or a jog? The hardest part is to decide to do so. It feels like an intense struggle to move closer to our shoes. But after the first step, our momentum moves us forward to step #2.

The math nerds will tell us, "If we don't get started, we have a roughly 100% chance of failure." Those are bad odds. So getting started is everything. How should we start?

"Thinking" our way to motivation is not a working strategy. Here is a test to check.

Q. Which is stronger? Willpower or procrastination?

A. Let me think about it.

Okay. We've got our answer.

Let's look at one solution to this "thinking" problem.

THE 5 SECOND RULE.

Okay, it is not an official government rule, but it should be.

A few years ago, Mel Robbins wrote the book, *The 5 Second Rule*. We recommend reading the book. Why?

Because motivation requires that we get into action. And it only takes five seconds. Here is how it works.

We have a goal and think, "Hey, I want to take action."

Mel says if we don't take immediate action in 5 seconds, our brain will kill the motivation. Our brain protects us from risk. She recommends instant action. And that means physical action. Get up. Move an arm. Pick up the phone. Put on our jogging shoes.

We will pressure our lazy brain by counting backwards: "5-4-3-2-1."

Action beats thinking. In five seconds, we launch ourselves into action.

But the skeptic in us thinks, "Sounds good. But what if I rush into the wrong activity? I don't want to motivate myself if I am pointing in the wrong direction."

Relax. Once we are in action, it is easier to stay in action. We can adjust. We can steer our action into the right direction if needed. And think about this. Most of the time we know exactly what we need to do. Our problem is getting started. I am sure that we will be "right" more than 50% of the time. That is a win.

Now, the skeptic in us might think, "This feels so artificial."

So what? Artificial can work. We buy special clothes or rent fancy cars to impress others. That is artificial. We have to get into action.

Try it. Take Mel's advice. Say, "5-4-3-2-1." See if your next task is easier to start.

This works. Just get up and move. Get off the sofa, even if to walk to the kitchen for more snacks.

One word of caution. This is great for reaching our positive goals. Don't use this technique every time we want to eat donuts. Or ice cream. Or pizza.

How about the long-term effects of using this method?

Mel suggests this technique will change our lives. Every time we use this technique, we are building a habit of action. That is a great habit to have.

THE TWO-MINUTE RULE.

David Allen, author of *Getting Things Done® (GTD®)*, has a two-minute rule. I love his rule because it keeps me from storing email messages that I plan to get back to later. The rule?

"If it takes less than two minutes, then do it now."

This simple change keeps me from accumulating stuff to do later. My default is to put things on my "To Do" list. I am a compulsive list maker. The result? I have pages and pages of things on my "To Do" list.

In our lives, later never seems to come. We don't have time. New stuff accumulates as we read this sentence. It is too much effort to go back to our old stuff, and then recreate the background and thinking for that task.

We should ask ourselves, "Can I do this task in less than two minutes?"

If we can, do it now. We won't waste precious brain cycles putting it on a "To-Do" list with the other hundreds of unfinished tasks.

Some examples of where we could use this two-minute thinking?

- Cleaning up a small mess.
- Returning a message with a phone call instead of spending 20 minutes writing an email reply.

- Putting something on the stove so we have something to eat tonight.
- Walking up three flights of steps at work instead of taking the elevator.
- Opening the spreadsheet and putting in some tax data.
- Organizing our desk.

My friend, Sue Mazza, had a "just fold five" rule. Her laundry machines were in her basement. Every time she visited her basement, she folded five pieces of clothing before going upstairs. Over time, the laundry folding problem went away.

In two minutes, the unpleasant task is off our minds, never to return. Yes, it is easy to put off unpleasant short tasks. But, it is almost as easy to do the tasks immediately and free our minds from them.

How could I use this rule? After eating my daily pizza buffet lunch, my next two minutes could be:

- Walk next door to the gym. (30 seconds)
- Buy a chilled energy drink. (30 seconds)
- Drink my chilled energy drink while standing on their treadmill. (One minute)

What are the odds that I will be motivated to take at least a few steps on the treadmill? Pretty good.

My mental toughness can last two minutes. Nothing too strenuous. Drinking a chilled energy drink is my biggest effort. But I am in motion. And my environment is perfect to continue to exercise.

Want to feel even better?

Clutter gives us an overwhelmed feeling. Another strategy is to remove some of our clutter. This gives us hope and a bit of confidence. Here is a ruthless way of removing clutter from our checklists. Eliminate:

- Things that others can do.
- Things that are outside of our skillsets.
- Things that violate our values.
- Activities that don't further our mission.
- Items that don't fit our current situation.

Deleting things from our "To Do" list may not be accomplishing things, but it will make us feel better about moving forward on tasks we need to do now.

A smaller "To Do" list is not so intimidating. Any little edge we can get helps.

MOVE THE TARGET.

Consider this "conversation" with our dog:

  We say: "Why don't you plan ahead?"

  Our dog thinks: "Pet me."

  We say: "Don't you ever think about the future?"

  Our dog thinks: "Future? Huh? Let's play fetch with this stick."

  We say: "You never think of the future?"

  Our dog thinks: "Scratch me behind my ears. It makes my hind leg twitch."

  We say: "Surely you have some concept of the future. You bury your bones."

  Our dog thinks: "I am selfish. I hate that evil cat. It steals everything. I have to hide my bones from that plotting, sinister cat."

  We say: "So no thoughts of the future. You're only thinking of now?"

  Our dog thinks: "I bet you have doggy treats. Give me a treat. I will sit up and beg."

  We say: "So no goals for tomorrow?"

  Our dog thinks: "Focus. Try to focus. Think doggy treats."

Yes, dogs have poor listening skills. But they have mastered how to live in the present. Only humans waste precious time thinking about the future. We worry about the future, plan for the future, protect ourselves for the future, but we can only live in the present!

That vague future.

50,000 years ago, humans worried less about the future and focused on the present. It was very important to avoid becoming lunch for predators. Worrying about the future is only a recent development. And we are not very good at it.

The future doesn't feel as real as the current moment. The future feels further away and less urgent. That is one reason we can't motivate ourselves. If our goal is too far into the future, it loses its power to make us act.

That is why we will change the game. Instead of thinking about our long-term, final goal, let's take some advice from our dogs. There is power in the present. How does this translate in real life?

Instead of thinking of our ultimate final goal, let's think of what our goal would be ... one minute from now. Yes, only one minute. That almost feels like the present.

- Instead of jogging a mile, make our ultimate, 60-second goal to stand at our front door with our running shoes on.
- Instead of losing ten pounds this month, eat a low-calorie snack immediately to ruin our appetite before our next meal.
- Instead of studying for our final exam next week, read one page of our textbook now.

- Instead of meditating for 20 minutes, close our eyes for one minute.

"Now" works better with our brains.

Future Me will become Present Me.

Here is proof that humans give more weight to the present than the future.

Imagine we are watching television, chatting at a party, or hanging out with friends. It is getting late. Do we stop our current fun? Do we tell ourselves to go to bed and sleep so we will wake up refreshed in the morning?

We may tell ourselves that we should go to bed on time, but Present Me takes over our minds and says, "Tomorrow morning? That is a problem for Future Me. Let's continue having fun."

Sound familiar?

And the next morning our Future Me is now our Present Me. Our Present Me groans, "I will never do that again. What a headache!" And our subconscious mind laughs at our good intentions. We can expect to repeat this performance again and again.

Have we ever tried to diet? Present Me wants to eat now. The extra weight we will gain is a problem for Future Me.

And we do this again and again and again.

Is it time for our annual physical? We eat healthy the day before the physical, instead of in the weeks or months leading up to the appointment.

Maybe we're expecting to play sports at the annual company picnic. We exercise in preparation ... the day before.

Our future goals fail to help us overcome our procrastination.

This is why we must shift our focus to short-term goals. Motivation is easier in the present.

So think about the tasks that don't motivate us. What would be our first step? Where do we wish to be one minute from now? And then make that step the goal.

Let's make this first step easy. How? By making the first tiny step enjoyable. This puts our motivation hormones on our side.

These steps will help us avoid procrastination and put motivation on our side.

There is an old saying: "The reward should be in the work, not the final goal."

This moves our focus to now. We can instantly enjoy the present.

And our final goal? We get closer with every motivated minute of action we take now.

IMMEDIATE GOALS VS. FUTURE GOALS.

It's Monday morning. The ladder-climbing corporate assistant manager returns from the motivational guru hype weekend and thinks,

"Wow, what a great motivational weekend. Yes, it did cost $10,000, but wow! I am a motivation machine. I am ready to face the fear, defeat my doubts, aspire to greatness, create my vision, chant my affirmations, change my life, conquer the universe, and drink ultra-caffeinated coffee until my eyes bulge. Bring on the world!"

Perfect.

And now it is time to take his first step, to make the first phone call to an unsatisfied customer.

And …

Something doesn't feel right. He thinks,

- Am I missing the best words to say first?
- What if my boss thinks that I am crazy?
- I did get rejected before.
- Let me freshen up my coffee.
- Is it time to check my email?
- Do I have any social media messages?
- Should I prepare for any and all objections first?

- Why don't I feel good about this?
- Why is my brain screaming for me to wait?

The assistant manager groans and says, "Uh, maybe I will do these phone calls later."

This is normal.

As we learned earlier, our brains are terrible with long-term goals. The further the activity or reward is in the future, the less important it becomes.

What about us? Have we done this before?

We make our weekend goal to reinvent ourselves. Our brain yawns and thinks, "What is going on in the next few seconds? Probably something more interesting." Our motivation fades.

Our brains look for social media scrolling time, snacks, television shows, or any distraction possible. We suffocate the life out of our motivation, stomping on any surviving flicker.

The solution?

Micro-chunking.

Micro-chunking means taking a big scary task that is far off in the future, and replacing it with a series of tiny but progressive steps.

Here is an example of micro-chunking.

Instead of worrying about the big, final goal of losing weight, let's identify a small step we can take regularly. This can work for weight loss, cash flow, early retirement, exercise, or whatever scares us. An example?

Late-night snacks are destroying our waistline. But we feel hungry before bedtime. If we eat more at dinner, we should remain satisfied longer. Our micro-chunking step is to eat another filling bite or two when we're finishing our dinner. We tell ourselves, "Instead of eating late tonight, let me fill up with a few more bites now."

Eating more. That works. An easy first step for us. Just another bite or two of filling food at dinner. We know the future will take care of itself. When we discontinue our late-night eating, our bodies will take the first tiny step to our weight-loss goal. All we have to focus on is eating that extra bite or two of food at dinner.

"A journey of 1,000 miles starts with a single step."

Let's remember the "single step" part of this famous quote.

WHAT TO DO BEFORE BED.

One of the biggest factors of procrastination is not knowing what to do next. Here is one way to tell our minds what to do next.

We put our subconscious mind to work. While we sleep at night, our subconscious mind is not sleeping. It is sorting information and new things that we learned during the day.

Let's imagine that we have a problem. We don't know what our next step should be. Instead of stressing about it during our day, let's turn the problem over to our subconscious minds to work on while we sleep.

While we sleep, our subconscious minds can search for ideas, try different combinations of possibilities, and often have a solution the next morning. Not always, but often. So why not take advantage of this free labor from our subconscious minds?

Here is an example of this technique in action.

We have a huge homework assignment. Where do we start? What do we do first? Are we going in the right direction? These questions dominate our minds.

Before going to bed in the evening, we pose this question to our subconscious mind: "What is an easy first step that I can take for this assignment?" Think about this for a moment. Let the question sink in. And then? Go to sleep.

There is a good chance that we will have a great first step in mind when we wake up the next morning. Because this first step is easy, and we feel certain about it, our motivation to get into action increases. Uncertainty is our enemy.

This seems to work best when we limit our subconscious mind suggestions to one request. We want our subconscious mind to focus on our one big obstacle to getting into action.

When we take our first step, the next step is easy. Objects in motion tend to stay in motion.

USING WILLPOWER
FOR MOTIVATION.

Just kidding. Nothing to see here. Let's move on.

We have to be delusional to leave our motivation to willpower. In a survey of 100 dieters, the question asked was, "How has willpower contributed to your weight loss?" The most common answer? The dieters left the answer blank. It took too much effort to answer the question.

What do we mean by willpower?

Willpower: "The ability to resist that second slice of pizza."

This has never been observed by scientists in reality. Willpower is a myth.

Science supports this conclusion.

For every person who claims to have lost weight using willpower, there are 10,000 people who successfully avoid losing weight using the same mythical willpower concept.

Accept our fate. We need shortcuts, tricks, and secret formulas to achieve the motivation we desire. This is the price of being human.

HANG AROUND MOTIVATED PEOPLE. IT RUBS OFF.

- If we hang around four drunk people, chances are we will become drunk #5.
- If we eat chips with four other couch potatoes, we become couch potato #5.
- If we hang around four negative complainers by the coffee machine at work, chances are we will become complainer #5.

See the pattern? Other people rub off on us.

Humans have a mind program that tells us to fit in, to be the same as others in our tribe. How did we get this mind program?

This program comes from our ancestors thousands of years ago. If they didn't get along with their tribe, they got kicked out. It was hard to survive then. Getting kicked out meant almost certain death. Yes, our ancestors were good at fitting in with the tribe. They survived and passed that program down to us.

So let's look around. Who do we hang around with? This can help us.

- If we hang around four people who exercise daily, we tend to exercise also. That gives us something in common.
- If we hang around four people who live below their income, save money, and invest responsibly, it will be easier for us to do the same.

- If we associate with people who take action and take responsibility for their lives, we will feel better if we do the same.

- If we hang around fit people who eat healthy, chances are that we will spend less time in the processed snack section of our supermarket.

Let's take a sample inventory of close friends.

Friend #1: Useless brother-in-law. He can tell us every new television show and the entire plot of each. He loves watching the stress and drama of make-believe lives.

Friend #2: The master-slacker at work. She prides herself on doing the absolute minimum to earn her paycheck. She boasts about how she gets paid as much as the hard workers.

Friend #3: Our overweight, donut-filled neighbor. He only gets motivated when he is calling for donut and pizza home delivery. He constantly talks about the latest food services.

Friend #4: Our party-addicted high school best friend. He congratulates himself on reading zero books since his graduation. He has a goal to sleepwalk through life on autopilot.

This isn't looking good. Our outside influences feel overwhelming. What action should we take?

There is an old saying, "If we can't change our friends, then get different friends."

Now is a good time to create some new associations. We should have a good idea of the types of new friends we want. We want to seek out people with good habits that will rub off on us. This will make it easier for us to get motivated.

Need more proof about associations? Think about kids. They avoid de-motivating adult associations.

Listen to them when they talk to each other:

> The older child says: "Adults? Stay away from them. They are energy-sucking vampires that hold us back."

> The younger child says: "Oh my!"

> The older child says: "Adults tell us to sit, to wait, to behave to their standards, and they never want to play with us. They are boring. Just avoid them."

> The younger child says: "Okay. Good advice."

> The older child says: "If we want to talk about negative vibes, adults are always saying words such as 'don't' and 'stop' and 'no.'"

> The younger child says: "You're right! They always tell me I can't do things."

> The older child says: "And avoid growing old or you will end up just like them!"

> The younger child says: "I never knew adults were such terrible influences on my life."

More proof of the power of association? Go to the weekend football game. Watch ordinary people lose their minds. They wear makeup with the team colors. Scream at the top of their lungs. Jump out of their seats. Associations matter.

What if our new associations encouraged us, told us we were awesome, and believed we could accomplish anything? What if they encouraged us to set even higher goals? Wouldn't that help motivate us to get into action? We get more confidence when others have confidence in us. This is the support group we should strive for.

But, what if we can't, or don't want to ease back on our current friendships? Then let's look at this strategy next.

ACCOUNTABILITY PARTNERS.

An eerie silence. Thousands of graves containing hopes, dreams, intentions, and ambitions. The stench of failure overwhelms us.

We have entered the "Valley of Failed Intentions." This is where our good intentions go to die. The valley reminds our subconscious minds that we consistently fail to get started.

Our solution? Time to reach out for serious help. Let's call our upbeat friend who oozes motivation. Let's allow some of that magic to rub off on us. It works! Yeah! Congratulations to us.

But we can't keep calling our one upbeat friend. That person will sense a pattern after our tenth call in a week. Instead, let's make a deal. Let's get an accountability partner. A partner gives us courage. Two is better than one.

What is an accountability partner?

Someone we report our progress to. And to make this arrangement mutually beneficial, they report to us also.

Things get done if we know we have to report our results to someone. The thought of reporting prompts us into action. We can't make up excuses in our heads where no one notices. When we report our results, others know.

Are accountability partners like mentors? No, no one is teaching or telling us what to do. We don't have to pay someone hundreds of dollars to tell us what to do. We already know what to do. Our problem is that we aren't doing it.

Are accountability partners like coaches? No, no one is shouting inspirational quotes in our ears.

Think of accountability partners as equals. We both know what to do. We both want to take action. And we both know that we don't want to let our partner down. We will do more to avoid disappointing others than we will do for ourselves.

Here is an example of accountability partners.

Keith runs. Keith would love to run every day, but some days it feels better to relax and be lazy. Who did Keith pick for an accountability partner? His daughter, Ella. They made a goal to run together every day for 100 days. Neither would let the other have an off-day. They did their 100 days in a row because neither wanted to let the other down. Rainy days? Cold days? Didn't matter. They pushed each other to their 100 consecutive days.

Me? I fight fat. Full-time. I am a magnet for calories. And exercise? No. The thought of exercise raises my heart rate to dangerous levels. I start breathing like an asthmatic whale. This is before I even leave the sofa!

Eating food in moderation is my strategy for weight maintenance. If I didn't have a diet accountability partner, I would be having this conversation daily:

I say: "Those dozen donuts look delicious."

The donuts say: "Have a few. No one is looking."

I say: "I want to control my weight. I will activate my willpower. Is that donut over there coated in chocolate mousse?"

The donuts say: "No one will know. Go ahead. Eat the chocolate mousse donut, and wash it down with the strawberry shortbread one. It isn't very big."

I say: "Well, you are right. It is only me here with the donuts. And I don't feel like exercising. Might as well have a few donuts. But I will balance them out with a diet soda."

The donuts say: "You had a hard day. Go sit on the sofa. Get comfortable. Take this whole box with you. You will feel better."

I say: "I like how you think."

And that is why I need to report to someone. I can't be responsible for dealing with my own delusional mind that imagines conversations with donuts.

Remember: Report, not reprimand.

I like accountability partners. I have several in my life. The motivation to report good results helps me when I am tempted to procrastinate.

Accountability partners are supportive. They don't judge, reprimand, embarrass, or make us feel bad. They are not our parents. They are not our bosses. This is voluntary. We are reporting to a friend.

My daily diet accountability call goes something like this.

I say: "I weighed myself this morning. Same weight as yesterday."

My partner says: "That's good."

I say: "And yesterday I turned down that second pizza. I felt one was enough."

My partner says: "Great job! Yeah, I am sure that second pizza would have packed on some pounds."

I say: "How about you?"

My partner says: "Yesterday I had a salad, then alfalfa sprout snacks, and a cherry tomato for dinner. I am feeling a bit bloated, but I am sure that will go away. I am down 15 pounds now since we have been checking in with each other these last several weeks. Soon I will be at my high school weight."

I say: "I saw a new calorie-free dressing at the store yesterday. You ought to get it to add more taste to that cherry tomato."

My partner says: "Ooooh. Good idea. A little variety will make this more fun."

I say: "Catch you tomorrow. Today is my cheat day. But I will try to avoid the cake buffet."

My partner says: "Awesome! Talk tomorrow."

No guilt. Only positive accountability. We don't want to disappoint others. And that little bit of extra motivation might be all that it takes to get us to do what we need to do.

Business people create accountability groups for breakfast.

Most major cities have at least one breakfast club. Small business owners and entrepreneurs meet one morning a week to exchange leads for each other's businesses. The accountability? If someone misses too many meetings, or fails to support the other members with some leads, that person gets banished from the breakfast club.

So besides the penalty and fear of banishment, the social interaction is a huge incentive for the members. Humans love engagement.

The 10-Day Challenge.

We can find new social challenges every day. Some challenges require pouring a bucket of freezing water on ourselves. There are those painful push-up challenges. Or how about the 90-day weight-loss challenges? Ugh!

But we do the challenges. Why?

Challenges feel fun when we do them with others. We share a common experience of pain.

If we have a bad habit or a motivation problem, I am sure we can find a challenge to take on. And if we can't find an appropriate challenge, then why not start one?

Make motivation an event.

Don't-Put-It-Off-Forever Friday can be the most important day of the week for us. We can be ultra-productive, wipe out giant lists of procrastinated tasks, and feel superhuman for the week-end.

This will feed our motivational mindsets. A series of mini-successes will build our confidence. Then, good habits form.

"Don't-Put-It-Off-Forever Friday" could be a motivational mantra for our team or friends. What a nice way to enter our weekends with momentum. The social proof could make this more exciting. Our friends could post the tasks they finished on social media. This could stir competition, or at the very least, encourage people to join. No one wants to be the friend who didn't participate.

So imagine what our personal Don't-Put-It-Off-Forever Friday morning could look like. For example:

"I arrive at my work desk, which is covered with Post-It notes, documents, and candy bar wrappers. Now, I clear a space for my oversized coffee. My plan? Start at the bottom right corner so that in 30 minutes, I will at least have a space to rest my right arm. To make my progress easier, I turn off my phone, lock the door to keep out intruders, turn up my go-to motivational music, and charge ahead. I am now the emperor of my domain. I am master of the desk."

Well, something like that. The day could use more chocolate. If we get good at this special day, we can finish everything in an hour or two. Then, knock off for the rest of the day to watch the 24-hour Cat Video channel.

What if Friday is not our day? Then how about starting every day this way for 15 minutes? We are in charge of our routines.

THIS QUOTE ISN'T TRUE.

Have you ever heard this motivational quote?

"We rise to the occasion."

What does this mean? I guess it means, "We instantly acquire new skills because we feel motivated."

Uh, that is not true.

Instead, we should re-word this old saying to:

"We rise to our level of skills."

Lacking the needed skills could stop our motivation.

Here is an example.

The lion tamer at the circus gets food poisoning. We get named as the replacement. This is our big chance to perform. We are motivated. We are excited.

We will "rise to the occasion" and become ... lion food.

With no skills, no experience, and only motivation, this will end badly.

If we don't have the skills to do the job, our subconscious minds do everything possible to protect us. "Bring on the excuses!" Our subconscious minds resist actions that threaten our survival. Let's not expect to rise to the occasion and train lions or fly commercial airplanes with no training.

As we improve our skills, more action becomes possible. So if we lack motivation and are afraid of our first step, let's ask ourselves, "Do we have the skills to perform this task?"

If we don't have the skills necessary to do the task, let's make our first step to learn the needed skills.

We rise to our skill levels. The good news is that we can raise our skill levels every day of our lives. A great goal is to learn something new every day.

Now, we may be thinking, "What? Some motivational quotes aren't true?"

Read on.

THE DESTRUCTION OF GOOD INTENTIONS.

Now, there isn't anything bad about motivational quotes. They sound good. We want them to work. But if we pin our hopes on motivational quote salvation, this means we've forgotten about our subconscious mind programs.

Our subconscious minds protect us from taking chances. They keep us from attempting new strategies. We are alive now, so if we don't change, we will stay alive.

To keep us from changing, our subconscious minds talk us out of almost everything, usually with a negative, sarcastic voice. Even if we hear the best motivational quote in the world, a little voice inside of our heads starts seeding doubts, and … well, we know how that ends.

Some examples of our internal conversations?

• • •

Quote: "Just do it!"

The evil little voice says: "Easy to say, but hard to do."

• • •

Quote: "It is always darkest before the dawn."

The evil little voice says: "It is darkest as things turn pitch-black."

• • •

Quote: "Never give up without a fight."
The evil little voice says: "Save time. Invest the time in social media."

• • •

Quote: "Don't complain. Just work harder."
The evil little voice says: "Seriously?"

• • •

Quote: "What doesn't kill you makes you stronger."
The evil little voice says: "So this is how nature removes fools from the gene pool."

• • •

Quote: "We are unique!"
The evil little voice says: "Just like everyone else."

• • •

Quote: "The road to success is always under construction."
The evil little voice says: "Let's wait until it's finished."

• • •

Quote: "Fight like you are the third giraffe trying to get on Noah's ark."
The evil little voice says: "And how did that work out?"

• • •

Quote: "If at first we don't succeed, then try, try again."

The evil little voice says: "Life leaves clues. Take the hint."

• • •

Quote: "This too will pass."

The evil little voice says: "Like a kidney stone!"

• • •

Our friends will recommend these pithy quotes with the best intentions. But what is the reality?

We need help. We need more ideas. More strategies.

We shouldn't stick our heads in the sand and imagine that our subconscious minds are working toward our lofty motivational goals.

Or maybe our subconscious mind tries this trick?

We say: "Okay, be brave. Let's do it!"

Our subconscious mind says: "Wait. We haven't figured out every step yet."

We say: "I can learn as I go. I will get experience. Let's start now."

Our subconscious mind says: "You know it is safer if we don't start. Something bad might happen."

We say: "I don't care. I really want this. Let's go!"

Our subconscious mind says: "How about we pretend that we don't know exactly what to do? Then we can procrastinate by attending trainings and doing research."

We say: "Well, I should do it right the first time. Good point."

Our subconscious mind says: "And we can surf social media while we search for more information."

Our subconscious mind has years of experience doing this. We shouldn't underestimate our opponent.

SURVIVAL COMES FIRST.

The office lights dim. And what's that smell? The odor of a rotting corpse? The hint of a pine coffin? The fog now surrounds our desk. And from the mist, our vampire boss appears. We wish he wouldn't wear his "Ethics Are For Losers" t-shirt in the office. Then, his thin and bloodless lips open.

Our vampire boss says: "Are you motivated?"

We say: "Yes!"

Our vampire boss says: "Are you committed to giving 110%?"

We say: "Yes!"

Our vampire boss says: "Great. Now go donate blood."

We say: "What??? That is deadly math!"

Our vampire boss says: "Release your puny thoughts. Look into my eyes. Now, kiss my ring. And here is some relaxing essential oil of chloroform for you to smell and relax ..."

This is why we never have the motivation to leave our thankless jobs and take the next big step in our lives.

Another reason? Survival.

The #1 priority of our brains is to keep us alive, and to keep us safe from uncertainty and danger. Any new action or risk brings the dangerous unknown. We are safe where we are. We are alive.

This survival program dominates our decision-making. How many freewheeling people do we know who ignore this conservative viewpoint?

None. They all died taking chances.

Reducing risk, playing it safe, and never taking chances is our default mental programming. Motivation to do new things? No. Not a big driver in our minds. Instead, if we feel trapped in an unfulfilling job, our minds tell us:

- What if I can't find anything else?
- What if the new job is worse?
- What if I get fired for looking?
- I need steady money so I can eat.
- My rent is due every month.
- Danger! Danger! Uncertainty ahead!

Our brain has performed well so far. We are still here, reading this book. We should give our brains a passing grade.

Of course we wish our minds would tell us:

- Why am I staying here if I am so unhappy?
- What else could I do if I were not here?
- Do I have an aptitude for something else?
- Can I build a dream life?
- I am a free person. I can think differently.

We have to make a conscious decision to take on more risk to improve our lives. It's difficult, but we can do it.

Instead of demeaning ourselves when we procrastinate, consider that our survival program is working well. Our program is telling us, "If we reach for our goal, there will be pain along the way. My job is to keep us from pain." Yes, procrastination is the result of a healthy subconscious mind.

But we have yet another option.

We can change our viewpoint about our soul-sucking job. We can decide that our job is fulfilling and brings us great joy. After all, some people work hard as fishermen. Others go fishing for happiness. The fish don't care about our state of mind. We can control our conscious minds and how we choose to think about our work.

Our subconscious minds have reasons.

Our subconscious minds are not our enemies. When we act, there is a reason. Even bad habits have reasons behind them. This is how our minds work.

Imagine we smoke. Obviously, that's a bad habit. But what motivates our subconscious mind to want to smoke?

- This gives us something to do when we have stress in social situations.

- The nicotine makes us feel good. Bring on the dopamine!

- The deep breathing relaxes us.

- It gives us something to do with our hands when we are nervous.

Our subconscious minds are always trying to solve a problem. A pleasing behavior is a way to solve a problem – in this case, an anxiety problem.

Our bad habits have motivational reasons to exist. So instead of blaming our subconscious minds, we will want to reprogram our minds when possible.

ARE WE EVEN DOING THE RIGHT THING?

Tommy Lasorda had a 0-4 win-loss record as a major league pitcher. Yes, he never won a major league baseball game. Now, to get to the major leagues as a player is impressive, but that didn't turn out to be his real strength.

Instead, he became manager of the Los Angeles Dodgers and managed the team to 1,599 victories over his career. Did he enjoy managing a baseball team? Yes! He managed the Los Angeles Dodgers until he was almost 70 years old. He didn't need the money. He loved managing.

If we have no passion for our careers, motivation will be a constant struggle.

If we have passion for our careers, then we never have to work another day in our lives. Every day we end up doing what we would do for fun anyway.

One way to get into action is to find a career that is self-motivating.

- If business is our passion, we wake up on Saturday mornings looking for a great day in our business. We won't want to stay in bed.

- If sales is our passion, making those extra phone calls in the early evening is an activity we look forward to and enjoy.

- If cooking is our passion, working late evenings as a chef is exhilarating.

- If teaching is our passion, getting students across the finish line is like a high score in a video game.

Why work in an energy-crushing mindless job that we hate? Instead, find work that gives us joy.

Think of the billionaires who still work hard because they love their work. It isn't about money. It is about achieving our inner potential and goals by doing something we enjoy.

An easy question to ask ourselves is, "Am I moving in the right direction?"

The good news is we are in motion. At least we are moving. It is easier to steer a moving car than it is to steer a stationary car. We can change our direction.

SINGLE-TASKING VS MULTITASKING.

Open two books, side-by-side.

Read a sentence from the first book. Then, read a sentence from the second book. Continue alternating sentences from each book.

How does that feel?

Confusing? Tedious? Frustrating?

We can only have one conscious thought at a time.

So what is happening as we read alternating sentences from the two books?

Step #1: Clear our minds.

Step #2: Read and think about the first sentence from book #1.

Step #3: Remove the first sentence from book #1 from our minds.

Step #4: Read and think about the first sentence from book #2.

Step #5: Clear our minds.

Step #6: Try to remember where we left off from book #1.

Step #7: Read and think about sentence #2 from book #1.

Step #8: Remove the second sentence from book #1 from our minds.

Step #9: Try to remember where we left off from book #2.

Step #10: Read and think about the second sentence from book #2.

Step #11: Clear our minds.

Step #12: Try to remember … This isn't going well, is it?

We can only think of one thing at a time. Everything else must be delegated to our subconscious minds' autopilot. Imagine we think about our plans for this weekend while we drive our car. Yes, our subconscious minds are driving our cars on autopilot.

Dangerous? Yes. But we can only focus on one conscious thought at a time.

Take a look at our teenagers. They do their homework while watching television, texting their friends, pretending to listen to their parents, and planning for tomorrow's fun. Only one of these activities will be conscious. The other three activities will be on autopilot.

Is this productive? Unfortunately, no. Multitasking is like reading two books at a time. Very inefficient. Our minds tire. Our thoughts blur. Our motivation runs away.

While multitasking may sound like a good idea, it ends up with less than optimal results. It is like brushing our teeth while tying our shoelaces. Or, eating with chopsticks while lifting weights. Or filling out tax forms while cross-country jogging. It's just not an efficient way to accomplish what we want.

What about distractions? They suck the life out of our focus and motivation. The constant bell ringing from the ice cream truck circling my home keeps me from deep, focused work.

Life is distractions on steroids. Nagging pre-school children, 24-hour news, social media cat videos, fast cars, squirrels, and the burnt chemical smell of shopping mall fast food courts.

Total focus will make it easier for us to take action. Single-tasking is the answer.

We can turn this single task focus into a game. The name of the game?

Pomodoro.

In the 1980s, a university student named Francesco Cirillo struggled with his studies. It's not unusual for university students to struggle with distractions. Completing assignments was especially difficult.

His solution? Try ten minutes of absolute focus on one simple and clear task. To time himself, he found a kitchen timer shaped like a tomato. Italian food lovers will know the Italian word for tomato. It is "pomodoro."

What happened during the ten minutes of total concentration? Focused, productive action. Our minds find it easier to concentrate when we put a time limit on our efforts.

Over the years, the pomodoro idea has progressed to:

- 25 minutes of focused action.
- 5-minute break.
- Repeat.

Some people can do several cycles in a day.

We make productivity a game by forgetting our negative excuses. We focus on our task. Then, go! We press the timer's start button and let our motivation carry us forward.

And if this seems too hard or rigid?

Start small. Start with a smaller time segment. Maybe five minutes feels doable at first.

Worried about our other distractions? Remind ourselves that we can get to them shortly.

What is standing between us and starting our own personal pomodoro routines? A timer? If we can't find a kitchen timer, set the alarm on our phone, or find a timer on the Internet.

Making motivation a game may not work for everyone, but it works for most.

MOTIVATE OUR RELUCTANT BRAINS WITH TRICK CONVERSATIONS.

We have conversations with our brains all the time. Here is an example.

Imagine a discouraged salesman, fighting the Goliath Procrastination Monster in his brain.

The salesman thinks: "I need to call my prospects."

His brain says: "We don't feel like it."

The salesman thinks: "I have the 'Eye of the Tiger' and ..."

His brain says: "No, we don't."

The salesman thinks: "But if I make these calls, I can move my career forward."

His brain says: "Logic; nice try. Stay in bed."

The salesman thinks: "But I have a vision board!"

His brain says: "Look, we're still in bed. Today isn't our day."

The salesman thinks: "Well, I am afraid I will get rejected again ..."

His brain says: "You can't get rejected if you don't call."

The salesman thinks: "Good plan. I guess I will wait until I feel motivated. I will make the calls tomorrow."

His brain says: "You know, setting up a calendar reminder means we will have to get up from this bed."

The salesman thinks: "Good point. Well, I will try to remember tomorrow."

His brain says: "Sure. Yeah. Enjoy the nap."

Good thing our salesman felt too depressed to check his email messages. There was a notice of termination awaiting him in his inbox.

Instead of submissively chatting with our brains, what else could we do?

Tell a "white lie" or story to our brains. Describe ourselves in a better way. Our brains have many mental lapses. This one little "white lie" might slip through. Here are some examples of how we can describe ourselves in a better light.

- I am a better salesman today than yesterday.
- I am setting good examples for others.
- I am the person that inspired the Nike slogan, "Just do it!"
- I am an action machine.
- Others call me "the finisher."
- I control the next 15 seconds.
- I am the boss.
- Movement is my middle name.
- They call me the king/queen.
- I am a lean, mean, selling-machine.
- I am the epitome of success.
- I am a living inspiration to others.

Will this work? Can we trick our brains into believing this? Sometimes. It is definitely worth it to try. It doesn't cost us anything. We won't depend 100% on this method, but it can't hurt.

THE SNEAKY, EVIL STRATEGY OUR SUBCONSCIOUS MINDS USE.

Imagine we have a very important but unpleasant task ahead.

Our subconscious mind says: "Don't worry. I got this."

Suddenly, we get an urge to take on multiple, less important tasks. We get busy. We get productive. We bask in the glow of accomplishing unimportant things while avoiding our most urgent and important task. Final score?

Subconscious Mind: 1.

Us: 0.

Our subconscious mind smirks. "Look at all you accomplished! Reward time! Relax! Grab a snack! Rest a while! Scroll through social media."

Our subconscious minds will do anything to avoid starting unpleasant tasks. Delay. Distract us. Anything. There is no limit to how low our subconscious minds will descend to keep us from personal motivation.

How can we fight this sneaky, evil subconscious mind strategy?

Step #1: See it coming. Know this will happen.

Step #2: Keep our focus as we battle with our evil subconscious mind.

We think: "Let's do this unpleasant task."

Our subconscious mind says: "Uh, no. Here is something we can do that is easier."

We think: "Don't distract me. I've got to do this task."

Our subconscious mind says: "Well, these easy tasks would be more fun."

We think: "Even if I did these easy tasks, I would still have to do this unpleasant task."

Our subconscious mind says: "Well, well ... uh, uh ...."

We think: "I'm starting now! Let me crush this unpleasant task. I will feel so good when I finish that I won't even think about those suggested decoy tasks."

Our subconscious mind says: "But, but ..."

We think: "Back to Satan's basement! I am taking action!"

When we feel the urge to answer email, return messages, or organize our desks, then we know our sneaky subconscious mind is working overtime to distract us from our focused task.

It is hard having heart-to-heart talks with our subconscious minds.

WHAT IS BETTER THAN A PEP TALK?

Pep talk: Check.

Hype: Check.

Affirmations: Check.

Feeling phony? Check.

We try hard to motivate ourselves. But sometimes we have to go deeper.

How? Try questions.

Be the ruthless interrogator of our stubborn subconscious minds. Our subconscious minds have to listen. They have nowhere else to go. Yes, trapped inside of our heads, we now have a captive audience.

So what kind of questions should we ask? Start with these three.

Question #1: "Can I do this?"

We think: "Can I do this task?"

Our subconscious mind says: "Not sure. Wouldn't you rather be eating cookies?"

We think: "Nice try. But I can get off this sofa. I have proof."

Our subconscious mind says: "Proof? Bring it on! What have you got?"

We think: "Observe the facts! I got off the sofa yesterday and walked to the refrigerator for ice cream. Last week I got off the sofa to retrieve the television remote control. And today I got off this sofa to accept the pizza delivery."

Our subconscious mind says: "You should be tired from all that standing up. Take a 15-minute nap. What do you say?"

We think: "Back! Back, evil one! I will leave this sofa now."

Our subconscious mind says: "But first, does this task have to be done right now? We should wait. There could be something else we could do that is more fun."

We think: "I am setting my pomodoro timer now. Watch me. And I will keep resetting it until I am burned out."

Our subconscious mind says: "Yikes. This is serious. But do you want to start your tax return now? You still have four more hours before the filing deadline."

We think: "I am reaching for my pencil. Stand back and observe."

Our subconscious mind says: "But what if there are new cat videos on social media?"

We think: "Taxes first. I need to get it off my mind! Then … cat video marathon until dawn!"

And that is the first question our subconscious minds hate. Why?

Because if we don't have the skills to do the next step, it is an easy win for our subconscious minds. When we prove that we do have the skills, the subconscious mind loses that round. Time for the second question.

Question #2: "Will I do this?"

"Can do" is a skill problem. If we can't do something, it means we lack the ability to perform the task.

"Will do" is a mindset problem. We have the ability to perform the task, but our subconscious mind refuses to start. This is the more common obstacle. We want to default to something easy.

We know we should go for a walk to get some fresh air and exercise. We have the skills to do this. But it is cold and windy. Our subconscious mind programs are defaulting to staying indoors, watching television, and eating chips. Are we up to the challenge?

Our subconscious mind says: "Smell these chips. They're extra-salty. Better to stay indoors and eat chips."

We think: "Well, what if I take these chips with me on my walk, eh? Can't stop me now, can you?"

Our subconscious mind says: "That is cheating. No fair!"

We think: "And I will pack a few extra chips to take with me and walk further. What do you think about that?"

Our subconscious mind says: "Stop using my evil tactics against me."

We think: "It gets better. I will listen to my favorite music while I eat these tasty chips and walk in the fresh air. This is feeling good already."

Our subconscious mind says: "Fine. You win this round. But I will be waiting for your next motivational challenge."

Question #3: "Which motivation is the strongest?"

Let's ask ourselves, "Are we more motivated to do this task? Or are we more motivated to not do this task?"

The awareness that we have choices helps. We can look at our options and pick the option that serves us best. This way we won't automatically default to the easy option of doing nothing.

Let's return to our walk for fresh air and exercise. Ask ourselves, "Are we more motivated for fresh air, exercise, and tasty chips? Or are we more motivated to watch television indoors while feeling guilty?"

Okay, we enhanced the choices in our favor. There are no rules of fairness when dealing with our sneaky, evil subconscious mind programs. We need every advantage we can get.

"Are we more motivated to do this … than not to do this?" This is a good question to use often to make sure we have some input on our decisions.

Question #4: "Is this a priority?"

When we ask this question, we expect a "yes" answer. After all, we do have high expectations for ourselves. When we say the word "priority," magic happens in our minds. We want to take care of priorities if they are for our own good. We have selfish programs. We temporarily forget "Present Me."

If we still put off the task even though it is a priority, then we need to make the task smaller, or more immediate.

Question #5: "Do I know what my first step is?"

If our first step is vague, now we have an excuse. Take time to rethink our first step. Make it clear. Make it small. Make it easy. Make it fun!

No one gets excited about an unclear mission. We need to visualize completing our first defined step.

Question #6: "Is my first step too hard?"

Our first step might have sounded great when we planned it. It is easy to make big plans for "Future Me." But when the time comes to take action, we can feel the resistance from our subconscious minds. If the resistance is high, it's time to dial down the difficulty of our first step.

For example, our motivated "Present Me" plans, "Jump out of bed and exercise." Yeah, that sounded good at the time of planning, but our mornings don't start well. Maybe our first step should be to remove our covers and take a deep breath. At least we are starting some movement.

Question #7: Am I going to be better today than I was yesterday?

Our reaction? "Well, I guess I could be 1% better. That wouldn't be much of a stretch, seeing as yesterday wasn't that good." By asking this question, it feels as if we are proving to our subconscious minds that we can do it. That we can get started. It doesn't take much effort to say "yes" to this question, and that action moves us forward a little bit more.

Before we give up on our motivation, let's put our subconscious mind on the spot. Let's interrogate our subconscious mind and see if we can get some movement in our desired direction.

MAKING OUR ENVIRONMENT WORK FOR US.

In 1830, famous author Victor Hugo had a problem. His publisher wanted him to finish a book, but Victor's motivation was to socialize and go to parties. Why not? Our brains find parties to be a lot more fun. The story may have been embellished over the years, but here was Victor's solution.

He took all of his clothes and had a servant lock them up. The servant's instructions were to release the clothes when Victor finished writing the book. With no clothes, and therefore no way to go out and party, there wasn't much for Victor to do except write.

Can we use this strategy in our lives? I guess we could take this to the extreme and wear no clothes until we motivate ourselves to do our task. However, the neighbors might complain.

But could we give ourselves a two-option environment?

Option #1: Do our task.

Option #2: Do nothing.

Eventually, we will get bored doing nothing. Our task will be more interesting compared to doing nothing.

Here is an example.

Task: Mow our lawn.

We think: "I am supposed to mow the lawn today."

Our subconscious mind says: "There is a heat wave! Stay indoors. Save ourselves!"

We think: "I promised myself I would mow the lawn today."

Our subconscious mind says: "Time to relax. Let's give this motivational feeling time to subside."

We think: "I either mow the lawn, or sit doing nothing until I take action. No social media, no television. Nothing until I mow the lawn."

Our subconscious mind says: "What???? Are you kidding? That's torture!"

The clock ticks in the background. We feel our subconscious mind twitching, starting to crack under the pressure of boredom. We go for the kill.

We think: "And no food for me until I mow the lawn. I have to finish this before noon."

Our subconscious mind says: "Yikes! No food? I love food! I can't wait for food! Let's do this now so we can eat."

When motivation is the easier choice, our subconscious mind goes for the easier solution.

NEGATIVE MOTIVATION WORKS.

It isn't pleasant, but negative consequences push us to take action.

- We run faster with hungry lions behind us. Our subconscious minds get in sync with our desire to run.
- We pay attention to physical and verbal threats.
- Jail terms prevent us from breaking the law.
- Fear of embarrassment forces us to step outside of our comfort zones.
- We want to prove people wrong. We want to make them "eat their words."
- We want to regain our honor from a bad past experience.

The fear of loss is greater than the desire for gain. That is how our subconscious minds work.

Why is negative motivation more powerful than reward motivation?

Because we tend to cheat.

If we are in charge of our reward, we can stay unmotivated and tell ourselves, "Let's take the shortcut. Let's enjoy the reward now. After all, we created this reward challenge."

That is why donuts are bad rewards. It is too easy to just eat them.

When we are not in charge of our reward, we can tell ourselves, "Well, we didn't want the reward that badly anyway." And then go back to our default activities.

Reward motivation is weak. Negative motivation creates more urgency.

So, back to negative motivation.

An example of negative motivation to kickstart our imagination?

England is crazy about football. Supporting one's favorite football club is almost a religion.

Let's look at two football clubs.

1. Manchester United.

2. Liverpool.

An example of taking advantage of extreme football club loyalty to encourage motivation?

John is always late for work. Sometimes only 5 minutes, other times 30 minutes late. If John showed up to his job on time, his co-workers would be looking out the window to see if the world was ending.

Excuses? John had a black belt in excuses. Traffic, car repair, weather, family, neighbors, sunlight. The world kept John from arriving on time. John would only arrive on time for the start of Manchester United's weekly football match. For the most important games, John would dye his hair in the Manchester United's team colors. The most important event in John's life? Manchester United's game against their ultra-rival, Liverpool.

The motivation challenge is obvious.

Every day John arrives late for work, his penalty is to wear the Liverpool jersey for the day. This is borderline blasphemy for him. Even the thought of this induces a gagging reflex in John. And when he has to wear the jersey, we know his co-workers will remind him of his new wardrobe. There will be teasing.

Yes, negative motivation is unpleasant, but it is one more way to get us to change.

Enough with the negativity. This could get depressing. Let's move on to a more upbeat method to motivate ourselves to start unpleasant tasks.

LET OUR PASSIONS DRAG US ALONG.

My caffeinated friend, Ed, talks a lot. Outgoing? Yes. Social fanatic? Yes. Enthusiastic? Yes. Maintains a dozen conversations at a time on social media? With ease. He lives to connect with others. Then he talks, talks, and talks.

Ed doesn't need motivation to do his favorite activity, chatting with others. This is fun! The dopamine floods his brain.

But exercise? Boring. Grueling. Mind-numbing. Ed knows he needs to exercise, but exercising is boring.

Ed's new plan?

When he finishes work, he can only start socializing after he begins his evening walk. He can't wait to get home and start his evening walk.

First, he gets to chat with other walkers.

Second, if no one is available for person-to-person chats while he walks, he opens multiple chats on his phone while he walks. Dangerous? Ed relishes the danger. He lives life on the edge.

For me? Walking is an unpleasant task. Time-consuming. Boring. I don't see progress; I always end up where I started. I hear that walking has many health advantages such as reducing stress, burning calories, and staying fit. Those are uninspiring benefits for me.

Ed uses negative motivation with penalties. He can't chat unless he starts exercising. For me? Negative motivation with penalties feels like self-induced misery. So what could I do instead?

Like my friend, Ed, I need to pair one of my passions with the misery of walking. Then, as I pursue my passion, the walking will come along with the activity. But why risk this plan on only one passion? Why not double the passion so that walking becomes irresistible?

My first passion? Popcorn. I have a popcorn addiction. Each bite brings bursts of joy to my life. Forget the four basic food groups. Popcorn rules.

The smell of butter and salt awakens my senses. The taste of added sugar and cheese explodes in my mouth. I go to the movies as an excuse to visit the popcorn concession stand.

So now, I only eat popcorn when I go for my daily walk. I can feel the excitement build in me as I stuff popcorn into a giant bag. Do the other walkers stare at me and my giant bag of popcorn as I walk? Yes. They're just jealous. My bag of popcorn gets oversized for my longer walks. I look forward to my walks.

But I take no chances. I guarantee my desire to get out and walk.

My second passion? Neuroscience and cognitive psychology. I download a few audio lectures before my walk. This floods my mind with interesting new ideas to test. 100% entertainment while I walk and munch on tasty popcorn.

These two passions overwhelm any negative feelings about a walk. My negative subconscious mind programs against exercise dissolve when it hears the first popcorn kernel pop.

The result? I want to add more walks to my day.

What brings a smile to our faces?

Everyone has unpleasant tasks to do. We can't ignore the tasks, but we can remove our resistance to working on these tasks. Combining an unpleasant task with a passion is an effective and pleasant solution.

The question might be, "What is our passion?"

To find the answer, ask ourselves, "What brings a smile to our faces?"

Everyone smiles at least a few times a day. What causes these smiles? Our subconscious mind is telling us, "Oh, we really like this." Here are some examples of passions we could link to a task we want to do.

- The smell of freshly-roasted coffee.
- Cat videos.
- Golfing.
- Cooking shows.
- Arts and craft shopping.
- Chocolate. Everything to do with chocolate.
- Movies.
- Lunch with friends.
- Gardening.
- Yoga.
- Fantasy football.
- Dance classes.
- Fishing.
- Music.

- Photography.
- Puzzles.

Certain cues will trigger our motivation. For me? The sound of popcorn popping tells my brain, "Yeah! Get some butter and salt now. We are going to munch flavored popcorn over the next hour on our walk."

Look over our list of passions. What cues can we use to kick-start our motivation?

- Music. Do we have a certain motivational song that gets us in the mood for action?
- Does putting on our Pilates outfit make our metabolism increase?
- Do we start whistling as soon as we load the fishing gear into the car?
- Will we jump into action with this energy drink?
- Does the smell of espresso put us into work mode?

Let's use our conscious mind to continue to come up with new ways to challenge the programs in our subconscious minds.

PUTTING OUR MOTIVATION ON AUTOPILOT.

Who needs willpower when we can achieve tasks automatically?

Our subconscious minds do almost everything in our lives. We don't have to think about how to open a door, or even tie our shoes. These are automatic programs.

Think about our habits and routines. We brush our teeth before sleep without thinking, "Should we brush our teeth tonight, or not?" The decision is stress-free and automatic.

Our strategy is obvious. Identify our unwanted task, and insert this task into one of our habitual or automatic routines. If we don't have to make a conscious decision to start our task, there is nothing holding us back. Let's look at some examples.

Imagine that we hate making our beds in the morning. Let's create a new routine.

1. Open curtains.

2. Open windows.

3. Make our beds.

4. Choose clothes for the day.

If we can do this frequently, we create a habit. We will continue to make our beds before choosing our clothing for the day. While making our beds on autopilot, our conscious mind will drift toward the clothing we will want to choose. We won't even notice the unpleasant task of making our beds.

Do we hate studying or paperwork? We could try this routine to create an automatic habit.

1. Put on the coffee.
2. Move snacks from the cupboard to our desks.
3. Turn on motivational background music.
4. Three deep breaths and a smile.
5. Read sentence #1.
6. Read sentence #2, etc.

Do humans have a Pavlovian response to routine? Yes. It is easy for our automatic programs to do the same thing over and over. Routine can be our friend. Automatic routines free up our minds for other things.

Another example? How about our evening exercise session at the local gym? Let's create a new routine to overcome our hesitation when we arrive home from work.

1. Turn on upbeat music upon returning home.
2. Grab a cold energy drink.
3. Change clothes.
4. High-five the dog as we leave for the gym.
5. Meet up with our gym accountability partners.

Compare this automatic routine with the stress of this decision:

We sit on our sofa, feeling exhausted, with an unhealthy snack or two. We gather enough energy to pick up the television remote control. We slowly ease ourselves into a comatose slumber for the next five hours. And then we ask ourselves, "Should I go to the gym?"

Our minds don't have a chance. Our motivation to leave our comfortable sofa and to fight our procrastination isn't enough. We are the object at rest, staying at rest.

Of course earlier in the day we told ourselves, "When I get home, I will jump at the chance to run to the gym. Nothing will stop me."

If our sofas have more power than our good intentions, then we need routines.

WE HAVE THE BEST IDEAS.

How do we feel when others give us advice? Do we love it when other people tell us what to do?

No. We discount the value of other people's ideas. Our ideas are better. We trust our minds.

Imagine we have a motivation problem, but we are out of ideas. What should we do? Listen to others? Or create our own new solutions?

Create our own solutions, of course. Here is one way to do it.

Brainstorming.

Brainstorming rules are simple.

1. The quantity of ideas is important.

2. Don't worry about the quality of ideas.

3. Outrageous ideas are encouraged.

4. Stupid ideas give us new insights.

5. We can combine useless ideas with another idea to create something special.

6. No judging the ideas until we finish.

The goal is to find a new idea or way of solving our problem by creating many options and possibilities. We don't need others to brainstorm. We can brainstorm with ourselves. Let's do an example.

Problem: We have no motivation to get healthy. It seems too hard to do.

Action: Grab a sheet of paper. Sit down at the breakfast table and tell ourselves, "I must write down two ideas that can make me healthier before I am allowed to eat my breakfast."

Well, that is easy motivation. We love breakfast. We write down these two ideas:

- Stop eating donuts for midnight snacks.
- Wake up on Saturdays before noon.

They may not be great ideas, but they count. We've got our two ideas. Now it is time to eat breakfast.

We repeat this every morning for a month. Two ideas a day will give us 60 ideas on how we can get healthier.

At the end of the month, let's review our ideas. Some are crazy. Some won't work. A few have possibilities. Here are some of the ideas we imagined:

- Hire a personal trainer to do the workout for me.
- Go to a vegetarian restaurant once a month.
- Chant healthy affirmations.
- Put less ketchup on my French fries.
- Take a multivitamin.
- Enroll in a belly dancing class.
- Go to comedy clubs to laugh and reduce stress.
- Trade in my car for a car with a manual transmission so I exercise my left leg.
- Add flaxseed to my smoothies.
- Walk up the stairs at work when I go to the second floor.

- Take up knitting for finger workouts.
- Join the local health club and maybe get a date.
- Eat one apple before I start on my regular snacks.
- Remove the sprinkles from the tops of my donuts.

Now we have many ideas to choose from, to mix and match, and to inspire us to create new ideas. There are endless possibilities.

The bottom line?

We want to improve our health. Instead of ignoring other people's advice, we discover our own genius solution. A solution that is simple, quick, easy for us, and most importantly, our idea.

10 EXHAUSTION TECHNIQUES.

To us, the unmotivated masses, exhaustion happens a lot. It is a part of our daily lives.

Even reading the definitions of exhaustion feels exhausting:

1. A state of extreme physical or mental fatigue.

2. The action or state of using something up or of being used up completely.

Feeling tired and unmotivated yet?

These definitions are accurate. Exhaustion means it will be hard for us to be that motivated, caffeinated superstar we dream of. Reality can disappoint us. That is life.

What can we do so we don't waste this "down time" in our lives? Let's make a quick list.

1. Tell ourselves to meditate. This no-effort activity fits our no-energy state of mind. It takes no effort to close our eyes and zone out. Plus, we can tell ourselves we are doing something constructive. Meditation helps our minds reorganize, clear a lot of random mental trash, and refreshes us. Difficult mental tasks are easier if we meditate first.

2. Learn something new that is helpful and interesting. This tells our brain we are making forward progress. This could be a skill that we need for the future. And, as an interesting side effect, this takes our minds off our current exhaustion.

We can watch an entertaining instructional video instead of wasting our time.

3. Check out our environment. Are we exhausted because of where we are? Who we are with? The mind-numbing task we are doing now? Then a change of scenery is in order. For example, we visit our local donut shop. As we stuff down a dozen high-sugar donuts, we listen to the locals complain about life. We may feel too exhausted to walk home, or even to our car. Environments make a difference.

4. We can tell our minds this is "recharge time." When we finish resting, we expect our minds to push us forward. Yes, we can influence our minds by giving them expectations. Another way is to yell "break time" so we don't feel guilty about taking time off for our current condition.

5. Check our "fear of failure" programs. Maybe we don't have exhaustion. Instead, our mind fears failing in our task. In that case, let's remember to move our goal from the end of the task. Our new goal will cover what we want to accomplish in the first 60 seconds of our task.

6. Remind ourselves that even the best genius minds have to rest. We are in good company. This could be our prompt to prevent our brains from overheating.

7. What about physical movement, like dancing? Hey, we are exhausted, remember? Yes, when we move and get in motion, motivation is easier. But for now, we are trying to deal with our "stuck in place" self who doesn't want to move. We can attempt movement by telling ourselves, "Now is a great time to go to the refrigerator for some snacks." This isn't the optimal solution, but at least we are up and moving.

8. Are we craving an electronic pacifier? Has our Internet connection created an addiction in our minds? If so, we can tell ourselves, "I won't go on the Internet. I can only rest." Within a few minutes our boredom will motivate us to do something more productive.

9. Think "opposite" like Charlie Munger, the famous stock investor. He calls his tool the inversion process. Ask ourselves how to get the opposite result. For example, ask ourselves, "What can I do to make me even less motivated?" Then we avoid those things.

10. Be daring. A gallon of coffee? Espresso inhalers? Intravenous energy drinks? 100-decibel heavy metal music? Use these short-term techniques at our own risk.

We need good methods for kickstarting our motivation when we are exhausted.

NO MATTER HOW BAD THINGS GET, WE CAN ALWAYS MAKE THEM WORSE.

When things are bad and we are at our lowest, it will be hard to conjure up positive motivation. But what if we stopped comparing our current situation to our past? What if we used our current low point as the starting point for a new direction?

Zig Ziglar, Mr. Motivation, once asked his audience: "Can you do something to make your life worse in the next three weeks?"

The audience said: "Yes, of course." This was easy for the audience to visualize and believe.

Then Zig said: "Can you do something to make your life better in the next three weeks?"

Ouch!

If we accept that we can change our lives for the worse, then we also accept that we can change our lives for the better. So even if we are at our lowest point of motivation, we know we can make things better. This is not the time to give up.

Most of us are not professional motivators. We don't teach motivation for a living. The old slogans for motivation won't work for us. Slogans such as:

- "Face the fear, and the fear will go away."
- "The only way to conquer fear is to do it."
- "Reclaim your power by refusing to feel fear."
- "Just do it!"
- "Feel the fear and do it anyway."

All we want are strategies to choose from that can work for us.

In this book we looked at many different ways to kickstart our motivation, to make our first step happen. Will all of these strategies work for us? Of course not.

We should choose whichever strategies and ideas fit our personalities and styles.

So let's not procrastinate. Let's choose one strategy to make into a habit now.

Good luck!

Thank you.

Thank you for purchasing and reading this book. We hope you found some ideas that will work for you.

Before you go, would it be okay if we asked a small favor? Would you take just one minute and leave a sentence or two reviewing this book online? Your review can help others choose what they will read next. It would be greatly appreciated by many fellow readers.

More Books from Big Al Books
BigAlBooks.com

How to Meet New People Guidebook
Overcome Fear and Connect Now

Meeting new people is easy when we can read their minds. Discover how strangers automatically size us up in seconds, using three basic standards. Once we know how and why strangers will accept us, meeting new people is easy. We can control the outcome.

Create Influence
10 Ways to Impress and Guide Others

Influence gives us the power to affect others and our world. Yes, we want to be heard, but what is more important than being heard? Getting others to take our advice and solutions, and apply them immediately.

How To Get Instant Trust, Belief, Influence and Rapport!
13 Ways To Create Open Minds By Talking To The Subconscious Mind

In this book, you will learn easy four and five-word micro-phrases and simple, natural techniques to build rapport that you can master within seconds.

If you are a leader, a salesman, a network marketer, an influencer, a teacher, or someone who needs to communicate quickly and efficiently, this book is for you.

Public Speaking Magic
Success and Confidence in the First 20 Seconds

In a speech, presentation, webinar, or even a casual conversation, we have just a few seconds to prove we are interesting and valuable. How can we capture our audience's attention immediately? By mastering our first 20 seconds.

We can forget about fancy tricks, jokes and manipulation. By using any of the three major openings in this book, we can confidently start our speeches and presentations without fear.

Start SuperNetworking!
5 Simple Steps to Creating Your
Own Personal Networking Group

Whether you are a small business, a
network marketer, or a professional
salesman, prospects that have been
pre-sold by your personal networking
group make your business easy and
enjoyable. Forget cold leads, cold-
calling, expensive advertising and
lukewarm referrals. Leave the world
of hard prospecting behind and start
your own personal networking group.
Have your fellow members bring new,
pre-sold customer and prospects to you
weekly.

About the Authors

Keith Schreiter has 20+ years of experience in network marketing and MLM. He shows network marketers how to use simple systems to build a stable and growing business.

So, do you need more prospects? Do you need your prospects to commit instead of stalling? Want to know how to engage and keep your group active? If these are the types of skills you would like to master, you will enjoy his "how-to" style.

Keith speaks and trains in the U.S., Canada, and Europe.

Tom "Big Al" Schreiter has 40+ years of experience in network marketing and MLM. As the author of the original "Big Al" training books in the late '70s, he has continued to speak in over 80 countries on using the exact words and phrases to get prospects to open up their minds and say "YES."

His passion is marketing ideas, marketing campaigns, and how to speak to the subconscious mind in simplified, practical ways. He is always looking for case studies of incredible marketing campaigns that give usable lessons.

As the author of numerous audio trainings, Tom is a favorite speaker at company conventions and regional events.